The Art of Being Still

Katie Kircheim

BookLeaf Publishing

India | USA | UK

Presentation by *BookLeaf Publishing*

Web: www.bookleafpub.com

E-mail: info@bookleafpub.com

ISBN: 9789363317888

First edition 2024

ACKNOWLEDGEMENT

"We can only heal others as deeply as we ourselves are willing to go."

Sending love and gratitude to all the healers that welcomed me into their hearts and held space for me so deeply,

Rachel K.
Emily L.
Lynn M.
Emily G.T
Chassie C.
Anna H.
Julie C.

. . . and the many yet to come.

PREFACE

Katie wrote each poem in this book by deeply connecting to her past lives, ancestors, angels, and spirit guides. She uses her poetry to express the longings attached to her soul, to allow her body to heal. Katie combines her spiritual gifts and poetry in her healing practice, The Watered Soul, to help women connect with their spirituality and heal from grief, loss, change, and infertility.

Muddied Hair, Hands, & Heart

The medicine woman doesn't blow smoke or air just because she can. She moves with the wind's sway because she's the life and the earth. She sees all beings in shades of blue, red, and grey—the shades of hope, despair, and balance.

All her traits reflect her spiritual awareness. She sees others as if their skin were translucent and their bones were dust. She sees the shape and sound of their light.

She walks and wanders the earth, taking in the expressions of the souls she encounters. She captures it in a time capsule in her mind; only drawing from it and unearthing its form if their souls meet again.

She's not fire or wind, water or earth—she's universal.

She never looks the same when you meet her; she leaves invisible pieces of herself so she is known.

She blows air and sways with the wind; a dance of art and healing. Others come from miles away because they feel her air, and gracefully walk her way. She smiles as they make their presence known but she never stops her flow, for that is what they came for.

She tosses muddied soil in the air and blows it to the sky; burying her hands to feel closer to the earth's center.

They throw soil too, in celebration and harmony, dancing without music to the earth's song. As muddied feet and faces move past each other in sound and silence; a surround sound of humanity.

Her tempo and flow slows as she blows air and soil to the sky once again, and then lays down her body on the dry field alone.

With muddied hands, hair, and heart, she opens her eyes to the sound of the wind, recalling the presence of those only summoned in spirit—from the woman whose heart is clear and whose body feels no weight of skin and bones.

She blows smoke back to the sky as her final
offering, and releases the medicine she created
for herself back into the earth.

A woman of medicine all her own.

The Abundant Tree

I used to walk through the fields of death.
Walking barefoot towards an undying tree,
where I could sit and be still.

But the tree never wavered and never fell upon
me. It was strong and used the essence of the
earth to stay alive.

The tree absorbed only what it needed, never in
excess.

I watched from underneath as it replenished its
life back into the earth. It always seemed to have
balance, even though I lie unbalanced
underneath its stance. The tree never touched
upon death; it was made to replenish and renew
its life force.

As I stared up at its grand beauty, I realized that
I've been walking paths filled with an
unrelentless fear of death, when what I've truly
feared, was living an abundant hopeful life.

As I slowly moved my body from beneath the
tree, I left behind the fears of walking through
the fields of death; knowing the tree never

absorbed these fears as it only took what it
needed.

The Grey Fish

I've sung songs like this before, hurrying my feet through grey mountains but this time it feels different. The moss and tiny rocks get stuck between my toes but they don't hurt; they become part of me . . . temporarily.

The grey mountains have always been my home, even though the skies are always dark.

I walk this path between the grey mountains while my friends walk the open fields. The rock and moss moving in and out of my toes like a song.

I start to hum along to its pattern, as the breeze carries away my voice. I scoop fresh water into my hands and take a sip, while waving "hi" to the little grey fish.

They look so happy, even though my feet are dangers to them.

As I near the path's end, I squeeze the moss out from my toes and step onto the flat earth, while my friends emerge from the open fields beside me.

I look back at the path between the grey mountains and see the turquoise and white colored fish—colors awakened once again, as the dark clouds have cleared.

Shaded by dark clouds or bathed in sunshine, the fish were as happy in the grey as they were in color.

The tightened path appears difficult, but has the happiest fish.

The Bird & The Bubble

All the birds sing wildly even with broken parts.

I wanted to run wild with the trees and all of creation. I wanted to use the earth's elements to clear my skin and my aching heart.

But where is the wild when you live within the tamed?

All the bubbles I see float away; they were never there to begin with—an imaginary complex of soap and water.

A desire to float away, while bringing joy and smiles; only to be tamed again within a colored bottle.

The bubbles float in the wild, but are always recreated with a small breath; can't we all float and live again by means of breath?

Maybe living wild isn't freedom at all?

I wanted to live wild among the gregarious earth and watch birds with broken parts sing songs I don't understand, while they pop the floating bubbles whose existence is unknown to them.

The bubble and the bird may collide, but neither of them fall apart.

I longed to listen to the wild bird's song without noticing its broken parts, and watch bubbles softly disappear into the atmosphere; never feeling like the bubble has been lost.

I wanted to run through the wild to allow my tamed mind to recreate itself like the bubble, and learn to embody the bird's song without emphasizing my own broken parts.

The Lone Flower

If the flowers could speak, they'd tell me that
while the storm sweeps away some of the bunch,
it also blows new seeds into the earth.

If pain had a voice, it would sound like a
whisper, even though it feels like a scream.

All the feathers of a bird may land softly on the
ground, while the rest remain sewn tight in its
soaring skin.

A thousand years of sadness comes rolling to the
surface like a thunderbolt; jolting the system to
feel.

I'm more than what I used to be, but still made
of the same parts.

If the brain had a loudspeaker, it would tell
stories trapped inside a woman so wise, that it
ate her alive.

If the stories flew free, the bird's feathers
wouldn't be sewn on so tight. Her eyes would
find the lone flower standing still, appearing
more beautiful than the bunch.

A thousand years of wisdom, to create a
stand-alone beauty.

I'm more than what I used to be, but still made
of the same parts.

Beauty in the Eruption

As I step away to find the volcanic sand, I start to drag my hands through its body. My fingers become the maestro as I play unfamiliar songs into its form. It composes black-formed letters of a hidden language; a language I've known but never learned its meaning.

I use my movements to create a symphony of vibrant information; placing my trust in this part of the earth. Its form repels many but attracts the light seekers.

I remain immersed in its sensation as the chorus repeats itself to me. A string of symbols and letters that resemble what I felt in my body, long before I sat upon the black sand.

All the letters scatter into the sand before they disappear. I feel the symbols in my hands and hear its true sound resonate in my mind. The words of the steps I've needed to take, to create myself anew, and welcome my own language back into my body.

The volcanic sand's offering allowed me to hear my own notes, sharp and flat, but in a voice that

I could understand. Many repel its eruption, for its beauty can only be seen when you submerge into it.

The submersion allows the black sand to reveal its voice without judgment of its body; attracting the light seekers to see what is not easily shown.

Sprinkled Sun

I've joined the fish in their journey towards
warmer climates but it doesn't feel warm to me. I
keep trying to lift my head above fast waters to
feel the sprinkled sun stronger; it touches my
skin, but I don't feel any different.

Why does everything feel the same?

I allow my mind to focus on the surrounding fish
and recognize that they are sprinkled too, but it
doesn't stop their movement. I notice each of
their unique glow that the sun invites me to see.

Perhaps the sprinkled sun isn't meant to feel
different, but is meant to help me see things
differently?

I look closer at the spots where the sprinkled sun
touches the fast waters. Its reflective nature
resembles my curious mind.

I've always wondered how this movement would
feel among the fish, and now I understand; it
isn't the feeling they chase, but the unique glow
that their movements allow me to finally see.

Moss Covered Feet

I walk steps to Roman Empires, covered in moss but bound by strength. The path never seems to end, and the cracks on the cobblestones feel like home. I watch as eagle-like birds surround the empire, taking their prey from beneath my feet. I never stay still because they watch my movements too.

I breathe with ease, even as the prey is taken upon the broken steps. The ash from the wreckage never fills my lungs, even though it's in the air around me. There are escapes surrounding my ascent's rhythm except for the one I desire; an escape to a new empire.

I continue walking to my ascent through the mudslides and rain that never touch my barren feet. All the sounds I hear are home to me, but lack pleasure. The sounds of pleasure pierce my ears differently than most; when you can breathe too casily amidst a tragic beginning.

I keep rising towards buildings beyond the naked eye, as the empire swirls blackness around me. The escape I once thought to find above has revealed itself below my feet, stopping my barren ascent. My ears start to fill with the sound of the eagle-like bird's hunt for prey, my mind suddenly recognizing what my body has not—I've become their prey; a still body.

My breath is harsh even though my movement has ceased. As the predatory birds start their descent towards me, I hold my breath and leap into the opening; choosing to fall beneath my Roman Empire, instead of walking steps to an ascent with no destination; bound by my own strength and moss covered feet.

Loving Aromas

I've never wanted anything from anyone. It's the
sound of the wind that reminds me that the
earth's elements always give back to each other.

It's never the same way, and no one asks for it.
The dried-up river doesn't ask the sky for rain;
the trees don't ask the wind to carry their leaves
away. It's always welcomed and received.

I step onto the earth and watch its surroundings.
I see a meadow and walk towards it—the smell
is wonderful but the field is barren.

Another gift it seems, as I slowly sit and allow
the field to relax my strong body with its aroma;
my body lulled to sleep while my mind stays
awake.

I allow the scent to fill me up, breathing it in
slowly.

A chill runs through my body; a reminder that
I'm alive.

The stillness comes again, and my body feels
like a smile, as I see flowers in bloom all around

me; finally connecting the smell with what once I could not see.

I know that my presence in the meadow can remain still, only observed by the earth.

As I run my hands through the flowers and feel their life and radiance, I realize that I too, can send loving aromas all around me, even for those who need time and stillness to see it.

Returned Particles

I remember a time when we were particles.
Where hope was an everyday existence and
connections were daily.

I remember that energy moved us, and that's the
only way we knew how to float.

Floating wasn't scary or sacred, it was the
standard.

I remember loss feeling like opportunity, and
newness not feeling like exile. Everything was
connected, so we were never lost.

I remember that our particles felt comfortable
and pure. I remember how easily we gave our
particles away; they belonged to all of us from
the start.

The colors were never the same but they always
felt familiar—an extraordinary rainbow. I
remember that we all birthed each other's
particles; community was everyone without
borders, rules, or silos.

We all gave to one another because we were all
in the same vibration; that we've come from
each other. Nothing lost or gained, just shared
and returned.

I remember joy more than sorrow.

Particles we were, but joy we found. If my
particles are one with all things, then why do we
question it?

I remember that my particles are not mine alone
and we are whole and joyous beings. I remember
to return to the vibration of our innate particles.

He Calls me Jelly

He loves me for my fluorescent-painted skin.
Like a jellyfish wafting through the waters.

My insides are crystal clear for everyone to see.
He calls me his jelly.

It's not the transparency that he's attracted to; it's
the alluring color. It's hard to describe without
explaining all of the colors of the rainbow, yet
it's not all colors.

He loves to spin me in circles and watch the
flickering sun shift on my skin, displaying its
brightness under the moonlight.

It's not the colors he loves but the intellect of my
skin; it knows when to shine and it knows when
to take cover. It fuels my open brain.

He calls me his jelly and it feels misplaced; my
painted skin is clear but my lifetime feels short.

What's a lifetime of translucent beauty without
the depth of color?

If I had shade, I'd have the depth of a lifetime.

He calls me his jelly.
He never calls me by how he feels with me, but
only by what he sees.

I enjoy his company and surrender to the
glistening light created by the sun and moon.
Light needs darkness too, which is why I glow
in the dark.

He calls me his jelly.
The allure of the light attracts him once again.
My fluorescent-painted skin dances with the
light.

He calls me his jelly.

As the light dances away from my painted skin
and I return to contemplate my clear existence, I
sit and imagine what it would feel like to be
solid-skinned. No brightness or lightness to
carry me away.

Depth strikes me briefly, as I remember that his
jellyfish isn't all that she seems—even when she
dances alone.

She called me jelly and I stared at her
fluorescent-painted skin and embraced it.

For she once called herself jelly, and that's all he
could remember of her.

23

The Hanging Heart

She floats in clothes because it's all that she has,
while leaving behind drawings in the dirt of her
creative imaginings.

Her heart-shaped tooth wrapped around her neck
floats with her—a symbol of her longing heart.

She wants her drawings to be embraced by the
elders of her tribe as inspiring innovations, but
they are only used to entertain the children.

She uses her float to cry out to the gods to bring
her more than this simple life.

She asks for her markings to be blessed so that
her tribe may honor her brain as much as her
gender.

She has what I crave, without opportunity.

I have what she honors, with overcomplicated
structure.

She floats and sings so that she may honor her
brain's creative vibrancy without the true means
of creation.

She's held back by lifetimes. I'm held back by a life of opportunity.

She never cries, for she is grateful despite her hunger for more. She knows the gods will allow her creativity to live beyond her body.

She floats back to the drawings she left behind, using her wet hands as a paintbrush to create deep impressions in the mud—a new tool for her vibrancy.

She sketches symbols she doesn't speak and draws objects she doesn't know. She somehow knows these drawings are her offerings for her next lifetime.

She squeezes her hair into the drawings to complete her work, creating streams of splashed patterns.

She steps away and leaves her watered drawings to be absorbed back into the earth, holding her heart-shaped tooth floating around her neck.

Kissed Toes

I'm walking barefoot in rocky terrain but it doesn't hurt, it feels good. I can hear the children laughing, but I can't see their smiles. I keep walking to the path's edge that turns smooth; something to soften my rugged feet.

I've painted pictures of this place before with red rocks and blue clay. It never seems to capture its essence. Some say it's desolate, but I know it's divine.

I walk into my hut filled with antidotes for those who need it. I run my hands along the walls and feel an energetic presence in my body. I hear echoes of wolves and owls . . . some fear them, but I've grown to love them.

I see pure white light coming from the bottles placed in the sun. I sigh with deep gratitude for the ancestors who came before me.

I move back into the sunlight before the day ends and pour caster oil on my hands, applying it to my skin to absorb the day in my body. I hear the laughter again, and when I look up, I see the smiles of the children running my way.

One boy stops and rubs my feet with his hands
and gives my toes kisses. He whispers "I love
you" to my feet in our origin language, then
walks away with a skip in his step.

He honors my spiritual essence because it's a
practice we teach children from the womb in our
culture. I love and honor him just as much as my
own body and spirit.

I finish with the castor oil and take the path
back, with kissed toes and blessed feet until
tomorrow.

What if you made a pact with the Earth?

If you promised to receive its essence and strength in return for its natural energy, what would that feel like?

The body releases through its absorption of the earth; trembling and twitching away sadness to bring stillness.

The energy of birds, trees, and the deepest roots underneath the ground.

Allowing the body's blockages to release and open more profoundly; listening deeply for clenched off fears to find what's trapped underneath—a vision of a body that can feel everything deeply.

Bringing forth rivers of tears to express locked battles of loneliness, unseen spirits, and life force energy.

Allowing the shakes and quakes of the earth's energy to welcome your spiritual existence.

Bottled Feathers

The leaves are drenched in oils from grapes;
oiled leaves, ready for the extraction.

The smoke from natural hot springs was used to
warm the leaves. The body was bathed in rain
water while feathers were softly floating upon
the skin.

The earth's wind naturally blew away the
feathers, and bystanders grabbed them as they
flew, in hopes to bottle them up. The sound of
their cheers and silence healing deep wounds.

Once the leaves cooled, and the body felt ready
to rise, deep dance emerged in tandem with
sonic sounds; the body freeing its last blockages.

The leaves lay strewn on the floor among
energetic feet to stomp upon; a celebration.

Once the quake slowed, the bystanders cleansed
the leaves in rain water, as tears from the body
sent droplets of gratitude.

The leaves were placed in the river slowly, yet
all at once. Bringing dual vibrations into

harmony; absorbed back into the earth for
another body to use its energy to heal once
again.

Breath & Death

It's never about me. I've always wondered what breath and death would feel like. It seeped into my bones like water into soil. The feeling was expansive but the energy was close.

I never wanted to feel something so close to me. It felt deep and boiled my blood. As breath and death reside within us all, waiting patiently to be summoned.

I never wanted it to be close, but then breathing became difficult and stopped my system. I felt the discomfort so I pushed it away—I had so much left to do.

It yelled inside of me to embrace, let go, and understand.

But I never bowed to it for myself, only for others.

I sat quietly and felt the resistance in my gut.

Only to be reminded of its inevitability.

When I breathed deeply, it felt close. When I
breathed, I welcomed it. But the moment I woke
from breath, I feared it again. It was a colossal
feeling, trapped in an ending existence.

Breath brought reminders of life's fulfillments
and accomplishments that I may never attain, so
I pushed death away.

The resistance remained until I welcomed breath
and death again; a reminder to create an
authentic full life.

It was only then, that I was reminded to feel
breath and death close to my body—celebrating
a life fully lived.

The Tornado Hunter

The tornado stirs and moves quickly before it
vanishes. We track its entrance but can never
pinpoint its exact presence.

It sweeps over oceans and bodies of water and
gains something instead of sinking.

It whirls around without a direction, yet reaches
many destinations.

Its water doesn't feel like a refreshing mist, it
feels like devastation.

A being so powerful, and yet, others never knew
it was there in the first place; it never existed to
them.

It doesn't aim to reach its destinations, it never
wanted to be there but it can't stop its path.

Do we sit and wait for its potential path or do we
go out and hunt it?

We can learn why it was created and predict
where it may go, or we can shelter and allow its
unguarded path to devastate our future.

We begin to predict its uncontrolled nature so
that we can create a known path; no longer
watching it stir but becoming the tornado hunter.

The Art of Being Still

The art of being still is that you can feel everything.

I feel the fluid movement of the water around me while being drawn to the pressure above.

Everything I see glistens in blue from sunshine spiked water. The greens look brighter and the reds feel deeper.

A slow wave moves from the water and into my body. A movement that allows me to breathe again, as it gently guides me to the surface; pulling my chin above the water, floating without effort.

I see what appears to be a calm ocean. There is no surrounding scenery and no sounds to hear.

There seems to be a lot of activity under the deep blue water but as I emerge, I feel perfectly still.

I float in stillness with the calm ocean; allowing the submerged activity to support my thumping heart and pumping blood. It's the weightlessness

of the calm encapsulated by the beauty of
unseen movement.

I allow the weightlessness to slowly pull me
toward the shore.

I feel the cool sand touch every inch of my body.
I lie still for a minute to allow the sand's
presence to soak into me.

As I sit up, the crash of waves greet my ears. A
reminder that the weightless stillness has a voice
both above and below the surface.

I bow my head in gratitude and lie back down on
the cool sand.

The sunshine glistens from my weightless body
and floats me back into the love of the
surrounding water once more.